GW00640709

Herring Fishing
Banff and Macduff

*BF390 'Betsy Slater' leaving
Macduff Harbour c1920.
(Built of steel by John Duthie,
Aberdeen in 1910).*

BF552 'Xerantheum'. (Painted by Robert Andrew).
Built in 1902 by Smith's Dock Shipbuilding Co. and first registered as
YH675 'Twenty Five'. Sold to Banff registration in 1913 and renamed.
Scrapped 1934 / 1935.

Whilst we have taken great care in preparing this publication, we have of
course relied on previous historic information by others; we therefore accept
no responsibility for any errors or omissions.

Herring Fishing Banff and Macduff

By
Stanley Bruce & Malcolm Smith

Published by
BARD BOOKS
on behalf of the
Banffshire Maritime & Heritage Association.

© Copyright Stanley Bruce and Malcolm Smith 2011.

First Edition.

ISBN 978-1-907234-06-4.

This edition published in 2011 by Bard Books

on behalf of the Banffshire Maritime & Heritage Association.

All proceeds from the sale of this book will go to the

Banffshire Maritime & Heritage Association.

Registered Charity No. SCO40505.

<u>www.banffshiremaritime.org.uk</u>

<u>www.webhistorian.co.uk</u>

All rights reserved. This publication may not be reproduced, stored in a retrieval system, or transmitted, in any form or by any means, electronic, mechanical, photocopying, or otherwise, without the prior permission of the Publisher.

Printed by Peters, High Street, Turriff.

Introduction.

This book was inspired by 'The Book of Banff', which was published by the Banff Preservation and Heritage Society in October 2008. They asked me to write a section for their book about herring fishing in Banff. I prepared nine pages for their book, of which they used only three pages. I then thought, as there didn't appear to be a local book about herring fishing in Banff and Macduff we could produce a small affordable one of our own. Hence, the section on Banff in this book is an expanded version of that which I wrote for the 'The Book of Banff', which was only partly used. It was then complemented with general information on fishing boats, and a new section on Macduff written by fellow committee member Malcolm Smith.

Whilst there has been a considerable amount written about the herring industry in general, very little has been written specifically about Banff and Macduff, so this book serves to fill at least a part of that gap. I am also happy to announce that some of the old photographs in this book have never been published before, and for this, we are grateful to Elizabeth Young (Nee McAree) who sent us photographs which were taken in 1928 by her father John D. McAree of Stirling. I'm sure there are many more old photographs of Macduff around, and if you have any please get in touch as we would be glad to see them.

I sincerely hope you find it interesting.

A' the best,

Stanley A. Bruce,
BSc; I.Eng; I.MarEng, MIMarEST.
Secretary, Banffshire Maritime & Heritage Association.

Macduff Harbour, showing drifters and the Matje shed. (pre1921).

Authors Note.

We at the Banffshire Maritime and Heritage Association recognise that much has been written about fishing generally, but felt there was a justifiable need to tell the story on a local level with a particular emphasis on herring fishing, due to its importance to the area – hence this publication.

The book is based on considerable research and comprises of archive information, some of which is generally available to the public but somewhat scattered. In addition, I have used local knowledge during the research process and have been fortunate in finding reliable sources that were directly connected with the town and its fishing industry. I felt it was necessary to build a profile of Macduff and its importance to the fishing industry. This I have done without going into detail, but nonetheless it provides a snapshot of the locality.

Malcolm Smith,
Committee, Banffshire Maritime & Heritage Association.

Macduff Harbour 1842. (From the Ports, Harbours, Watering Places and Picturesque Scenery of Great Britain by W. H. Bartlett).

Herring.

Herring *'Clupea harengus' can* grow up to 45cm (18 inches) in length and can weigh as much as 500grams (1lb). However those caught around the UK are usually around 30cm long and weigh around 200grams. They are rich in protein, and have always been an excellent source of nutrition. In the early years, they were affectionately known as the 'Silver Darlin's'. Shoals of herring migrate along the British coastline generally from the north in the spring heading to the southeast coast of England for the winter months.

Economically, herring has in the past been the world's most important fish, and one of the earths most used marine resources. Herring being readily available was once crucial to the Scottish diet. Herring is an oily fish and it provided a cheap, plentiful, and nutritious source of food. They have been caught off the cost of Scotland for hundreds of years, and at least commercially by the Dutch since the 1600's.

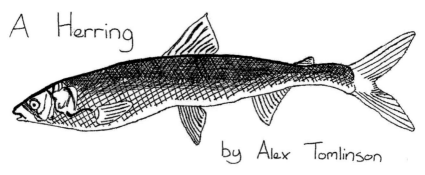

A Spent Herring. (A fish that has spawned).

Originally, herring were fished close to shore; however, from the 1860's nets got lighter and fishing boats started to get bigger, and as they did this allowed fishermen to catch more. With the introduction of steam engines, the fishermen could fish much further offshore and still be able to land their catch without it deteriorating. Herring once caught deteriorate very quickly and if the quality of the fish is to be preserved, they must be landed and processed within 24 hours.

The term 'Scotch Cure' was established in 1819, and Fishery Officers were appointed to ensure that the quality of the cured herring was high enough to be given the 'Crown Brand'. This meant that each barrel of cured herring was filled with a certain grade of herring and marked with the name and address of the curer, the name of the fishery officer, and the text 'Crown Brand'. This brand had a worldwide reputation for being the best. There were seven grades of herring, which at times took a bit of sorting by the gutting quines.

Herring Grades.

Name.	Description	Size
Large Full.	Big fish full of milt and roe.	> 11 ¼" long.
Full.	Fish full of milt and roe.	> 10 ¼" long.
Filling.	Maturing fish.	> 10 ¼" long.
Medium.	Maturing fish.	> 9 ½" long.
Matfull.	Fish full of milt and roe.	> 9 ¼" long.
Mattie.	Young maturing fish.	> 9" long.
Spent.	Fish that has spawned.	> 11 ¼" long.

Herring baskets were also marked with the crown brand, the date, and the fishery officer's initials.

A small sample basket was used to take a sample of herring to the auction.

Once sold the herring was unloaded from the boats in large baskets, which could hold 7 stone of herring. These were carted often pulled by horses or men to the farlanes to be processed by the gutting quines who worked in teams of three, two gutting and one packing.

Crown mark on a herring basket of 1900. (S. Bruce).

Fishing Boats.

Initially small open deck clinker built boats made of wood were used, and in the days before powered craft came along, they were rigged with sails and therefore reliant on the wind alone. Typical were the open-decked Skaffies, well liked by the fishermen of the day, but providing no shelter for the crew during bad weather or heavy seas.

Clinker Built.

The Skaffie was clinker built. This build method meant that the hull planks were overlapped. The relative cheap cost of building these boats made them popular with the fishermen. They were also light, which made them easy to pull onto the beach. As build methods improved the boats became much bigger in size, up to forty feet long.

Clinker Built.

Carvel Built.

When boats became even bigger, the hull planks became thicker simply because they needed to be stronger; this meant that they could not be overlapped as used in a clinker built boat. It was therefore necessary to adopt a different boat-building method where the planks were laid side by side (Butted together) and a caulking compound fitted between.

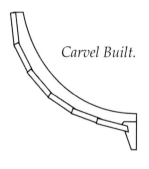

Carvel Built.

Skaffie (Scaffie).

The first boats used productively in fishing on the Moray Firth were the Skaffies; they were wooden hulled open decked boats about nineteen feet in length, and affording little or no protection to the hard working men who sailed them. The open deck was fine for the catch and enabled the men to fill the boat with fish – the downside of this was that the open deck was easily swamped in heavy seas, and it did limit the fishermen by forcing them to stay within easy distance of the shore. They were clinker built, initially with a beam of approximately 7 feet, however, these boats gradually increased in length up to 40 feet, with a beam of around 13 feet, and a draft of a little less than 5 feet, powered by two lugsails and handled by a crew of not more than five. These boats were usually equipped with two pairs of oars for use when there was no wind, and the boats could often be seen rowing in or out of the harbours. Due to the shape of their hulls, Skaffies were easily beached, as they needed to be, since harbours were not established in many of the fishing villages until early in the 19th century.

This drawing c1880 clearly shows small open decked clinker built boats in Macduff Harbour, with 26BF in the foreground.
(Copied from Johnny Gibb of Gushetneuk in the parish of Pyketillim 1881).

Early registration numbers as shown above had the number preceding the registered port letters.

Small herring boats on the Greenbanks, Banff c1900.
(Note Macduff Railway Station on the right, now Seaway).

The Skaffie was gradually replaced by an improved design known as the Zulu, which was a design comprising of the best features of the Skaffie and the Fifie.

Fifie.
The early Fifie sailboats were about the same length as the early Skaffies, about forty feet, however the Fifie with it's long keel was far more suited to the rougher seas with increased stability a feature of its design. They were certainly more seaworthy than the Skaffies, and the more enclosed half deck improved matters considerably for the fishermen. They were favoured by the fishermen of the east coast of Scotland.

The later larger Fifies were carvel built. These boats were up to 70 feet long, with a wide beam, which made them very stable in the water. Later models such as the 70 feet long FR958 'Reaper' were fitted with two masts, a mainmast forward and a mizzenmast near the stern.

Fifie herring boat - FR958 'Reaper', Portsoy Harbour. (S. Bruce).
Built by J. & G. Forbes, Sandhaven, and registered at Fraserburgh in 1902.

Zulu.

Fishermen on the Moray Firth favoured the Skaffie until 1879, when William 'Dad' Campbell of Lossiemouth developed the Zulu fishing boat. The first Zulu built by Campbell was named the 'Nonesuch'. The name Zulu was taken from the Zulu Wars, which were ongoing at the time in South Africa. The Zulu, which was built up to 80 feet long, was a more robust boat with a much greater capacity than its predecessors. It was derived from the best characteristics of the Skaffie and the Fifie, including full decking. The Fifie had a vertical bow and stern giving it a long keel, and was favoured by fishermen from Fraserburgh and further south. The Zulu used the raked stern of the Skaffie and the vertical bow of the Fifie. A wooden hulled Zulu drifter the 'Research' originally built as the 'Heather Bell' in 1903 by W. & G. Stephen, Boat-builders, Banff can be seen in the Scottish Fisheries Museum in Anstruther. The hull of another Zulu the 'Hirta II' can be seen in Macduff. It is currently sited on a dry berth at Macduff Shipyards, Union Row.

It would be fair to say that the Zulu was considered a fine boat by the crews that sailed and earned their living in them, and that it was well equipped to cope with all that nature could produce. Later in its development, the steam capstan was introduced making both the hoisting of the heavy sails and the hauling in of the catch far easier for the crews.

Zulu sailing boat 'Hirta II' on a dry berth at Macduff. (S. Bruce).

Zulu fishing boat in Buckie Harbour. (BM&HA).

Steam Drifter.

The most notable fishing boat that evolved from the Zulu, and which really made its mark in much improved productivity, efficiency, and safety was the much revered steam drifter. Its fine lines and well thought design were to be welcomed by all but the most stubborn of fishermen. No longer were the men reliant on wind alone, now they could sail further, faster, and bring in the catch to market quickly without having to worry unduly about the weather. Just imagine in the early days of sail having a very good catch only to become becalmed, and not get the fish to port before its freshness was lost. In the steam drifter the fishermen could steam in a straight line thus improving efficiency yet further - no need for tiresome tacking when the wind was blowing in the wrong direction. The steam drifter became synonymous with the herring fishing, for not only did catches improve, but the men had a better degree of comfort with a sheltered wheelhouse, a cabin in which to eat, rest, and sleep, in better conditions than they had ever experienced before. It was far safer too, and its ruggedness and stability made it something of a design icon. In later years, many were converted to diesel power, and most saw wartime service with the government of the day, under the banner of the Admiralty, enlisting them and their fine crews for active service, with many serving in WW1 and WW2. Wooden hulled steam drifters were of carvel construction, they were strong, and of course, they had to be. They could carry more nets, and catch and carry much more fish than their predecessors. The hulls of boats built in Banff and Macduff were built of wood; although some owners opted for a hull made of steel, and sourced a boat further afield. All of the drifters made in Aberdeen had steel hulls. Of course fishing with a steam drifter gave a higher catch rate and capacity, and it needed to, because the costs of building a steam drifter in the early 1900's was in the region of £3,000 to £4,000, which was about three times the cost of the older sailing boats. Due to this significantly higher cost, some fishermen were slow to adopt the new technology.

The increased length of fishing nets made the steam capstan a vital component in the construction of fishing boats. Some fishing boats built before the steam driven drifters had steam-operated capstans, but they still relied on sail-power. With the introduction of the steam-powered engine in the drifters, efficiency and reliability greatly improved. Engines were undergoing improvements all the time and eventually came the new fangled oil engine that we came to call a diesel. The first engines were crude affairs, but as with everything, they improved and in turn were more reliable, and perhaps most importantly had significantly reduced running costs. Better boats meant bigger catches, and whilst this may appear the way forward, the reality was that bigger catches brought the price down, and eventually lead to a glut, which did nothing for the industry and many observers, with hindsight, saw a decline in stocks. Over-fishing was a great problem for the industry, and some say it still is.

BF73 'Regent Bird'. (Scrapped in 1951). (Courtesy of James Gatt).

The 'Regent Bird' was built in 1909 by Alexander Hall & Co., Ltd., Footdee, Aberdeen (Yard No. 452) for George Murray, Buckie. Alexander Hall & Co. also built her 37HP, 18 inch compound engine, and her 130psi boiler. She was first registered as BCK49, and was a typical steam drifter of the time, she had the following particulars:

Length: 86.6 feet.　　　　Gross Registered Tonnage (GRT): 88 tons.
Breadth: 18.7 feet.　　　　Depth: 9 feet.

The 'Regent Bird' was sold to John West of Gardenstown, and transferred to Banff registration in 1946. Like most of the steam drifter's she served during both World Wars. During WW1, she served as a Boom Defence Vessel from 1915 to 1919, and during WW2, as an Examination Vessel from 1939 to 1945. Many other drifters were used as minesweepers or tenders; the 'Regent Bird' like all Aberdeen built fishing boats had a steel hull, and with the introduction of magnetism in mines during WW2 was not suited to being a minesweeper. However most steel hulled boats used by the Admiralty had a degaussing loop made of heavy gauge copper cables fitted around the hull and deckhouse demagnetising the boat and making it 'virtually invisible'.

BF45 'Craigalvah' berthed in Macduff Harbour c1930. (BM&HA Archive).

'Craigalvah' was built of wood in 1909 by W. & G. Stephen of Banff for Paterson, Macduff. Length 85.9 feet, breadth 18.8 feet, depth 8.8 feet, and engine 30HP. She served in WW1 from 1914 to 1920 as a stores and water carrier, and in WW2 from December 1939 to December 1945 on harbour service. She was scrapped in 1950-1.

Engines and Boilers.

Around 1905 / 1906 paraffin and petrol engines were introduced. Initially they were only fitted to small boats of around 15 to 30 feet long providing auxiliary power to assist the raising and lowering of the sails. However, it was not long before improvements to these motor engines led to them overtaking steam as a preferred option, not least because they did away with the need for a fireman/stoker and the fuel could be piped aboard, less labour intensive and far cleaner than coal and importantly cheaper to run. No need for three hours spent raising a head of steam. These new engines were favoured by most, although there remained stubbornness on the part of some to remain with the old ways and continue with steam.

As diesel engines improved and became more powerful and efficient, they took over as the main method of propulsion, and conventional sails were dispensed with. These engines compared to steam engines were relatively cheap to purchase, and were easily installed in the larger boats. Fuel costs were low, and the maintenance costs were considerably lower than those of a steam engine.

Engine makers Gardiner and Kelvin dominated the fishing boat market, and since they were relatively compact, they were fitted to existing Fifies, Skaffies, and Zulus; thereby converting them from sail to motor.

BF1411 'Norseman'. (Photographer unknown).

BF1411 'Norseman' was the first steam drifter built for the port of Macduff, she was built for J. J. George and others. She was built of wood in 1903 by W. & G. Stephen of Banff. Her gross registered tonnage (GRT) was 75 tons, length 81.2 feet, breadth 18.7 feet, and she had a depth of 8.8 feet. She foundered off Fraserburgh in 1912.

As steam engines developed, they became more sophisticated and more powerful than the 14 inch compound engine fitted to the 'Norseman', which was perhaps at the lower end of the power scale, with its 16 HP engine; for example, the later 16 inch triple expansion engine delivered 40 HP. The last steam drifter built in the UK, which was built by in 1932 by Alexander Hall & Co., Aberdeen (Yard No. 638) the 'Wilson Line' delivered 36HP.

Triple-expansion marine engine with gear-driven shaft. (Bartlett).

The most popular marine diesel engines used on engine powered fishing boats, were made by L. Gardner and Sons, or Kelvin.

L. Gardner and Sons started building diesel engines in 1903. Kelvin was much later with their diesel engine; it was not introduced until 1931. However, in 1906 the company known then as the "Bergius Launch and Engine Company" fitted one of its 14HP car engines in a clench built rowing gig, whilst in 1906 its first commercially sold engine was fitted to the 'Progress' a ferry built for Baltasound by J. & G. Forbes, Sandhaven.

Fuel.
Each steam drifter sailing at about 10 knots typically used 8 tons of coal a week. A typical drifter had the capacity to hold about 40 tons of coal, meaning it could sail for 5 weeks on a full load. Because of this need for coal, coal yards were established at Macduff.

Coal was brought to Macduff by cargo boat, and stored by Northern Coal and Lime Co., Skene Street (now Lyndon Court), Robertson adjacent to the Maritime Garden at Crook 'o Ness Street (Now part of Macduff Shipyards), and by Mitchell and Robb near the Aquarium.

Discharging coal at Macduff Harbour 1928. (John D. McAree of Stirling). (Note the buildings at Crook o' Ness Street on the right, now demolished).

Section through the 'Protea' a typical Steam Trawler built in 1938 for Irvin & Johnson (South Africa) Ltd, Cape Town. (Hall Russell).

The picture above shows the typical layout within a trawler with its copious hold, large boiler, steam engine, bunker area, and above deck aft the mizzenmast, which was so important in ensuring the trawler and its nets were kept in line whilst fishing. It truly is a wonderfully iconic design.

We cannot give an exact quantity of herring that a drifter could hold, we can however advise that in 1936, BF 592 'Boy Andrew' of Portsoy was the first drifter to win the Prunier Herring Trophy, and she won by landing 231 crans. (A cran was four baskets, and each basket held approximately 7 stone, which makes a cran 28 stone). Therefore the catch landed by the 'Boy Andrew' was approximately 6,468 stone, which is approximately 41 tonnes.

Drift Net.

Fishermen sailed to where they thought they would find herring, or until they saw signs of the fish in the water. Nets were put out, (or shot) at dusk when the herring were feeding close to the surface. The boat was swung head to the wind, the mizzen sail was raised, and she was left to drift, usually for most of the night. As she drifted, she pulled on the long warp rope so keeping her nets taut. When fish swim into the drift nets, the mesh allows an adult herring to enter as far as its head but when it tries to wriggle backwards, the threads of the mesh catch under its gills stopping it from escaping.

Drifter shooting her nets.

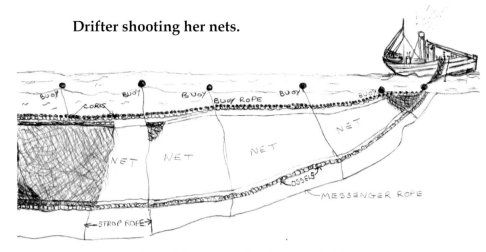

Drift Net. (Drawing by Kay Smith).

Drifter with her nets down ready to haul.

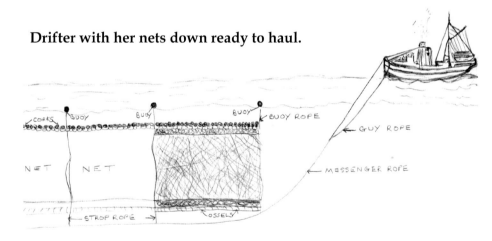

Drifter with nets down ready to haul. (Drawing by Kay Smith).

The drift net was made up of several nets (known as a train), joined in a line then hung curtain style just below the surface. The nets around fifty feet deep were supported just below the surface by cork buoys, and attached to the bow of the boat by a long rope known as the swing rope, which changed its name to the warp as nets were attached, this became known as the drift. The nets were shot at dusk simply because the herring come to the surface to feed at night. The drift train of nets when shot was allowed to drift with the current, hence the name. At the end of fishing, around dawn, the nets would be dragged aboard and the herring shaken out into the hold. This was hard demanding work as the drift could be several hundred yards, perhaps even miles long.

Through the years, drift nets have varied in size and material, but the principle of the drift net did not change. It was a clever design that allowed fisherman to catch the fish without the need for bait since the herring simply swam into the mesh of the net and became trapped by their gills. With bait no longer needed, that cut out a great deal of intensive labour, certainly on the part of the fishermen's wives. As the nets were hauled in the fish were shaken out onto the deck of the boat, with the net being coiled ready for the next shot.

Early nets were made by hand from hemp yarn by fishermen or their wives. Around 1850, James Patterson of Musselburgh invented a loom that was capable of weaving cotton nets. Whilst the size of the nets could vary, there were attempts to set a standard; the rationale behind this being a very early attempt at conservation, and a desire to allow small or infant fish to simply swim through the mesh. An essay written by C. W. Morris and presented at the International Fisheries Exhibition at Norwich in 1881, and again at the International Fisheries Exhibition in Edinburgh in 1882, sought to suggest a common policy could be adopted in regulating the mesh size, and at the same time a standard adopted for a complete net. It went thus: a single net should be 25 yards long and 3 yards deep with the number of meshes to the yard being 38. The essay also asked the question "Should the mesh size be fixed by law?" (38 meshes to the yard gives a mesh size of about 1 inch).

Originally nets were made of linen or hemp, however in the 1860's cotton nets were introduced, which were much lighter, and this led to the position of the warp (messenger rope) being changed so it hung below the nets. Its size and weight were important factors and a typical warp would be 3.25 inches in diameter. It was a tarred rope (tarry rope), and the cotton nets were strengthened by 'Barking', which was a process where they were soaked in an extract of oak or birch bark. Progress played its part and engineers developed a powered capstan to remove the hard work in pulling in the nets by hand. The capstan sat on the foredeck. Initially capstans were manually operated, but later they were powered by steam. Further improvements led to the capstan being driven by a diesel engine. The capstan proved useful in many ways, and certainly allowed much larger nets to be hauled. It was also used for raising the sails, making bigger boats with bigger sails a consequence. You can see at every stage of the fishing industry man's resourcefulness and invention has allowed continuous improvement within the industry. Hard to believe the humble beginning from small open-decked boats to today's multi-million pound fishing boats with their electronic gadgetry, and state of the art fishing gear, yet they still rely on the humble or should I say noble fishermen to bring it all together. Fishing is often described as the most dangerous job in Britain, even with all this new technology perhaps it still is!

Floats.
Early floats were made from cork, glass, and cow or in some more unsavoury cases dog bladders.

BF336 'Milky Way' and BF103 'Token', Macduff Harbour. (Courtesy J. Gatt).

Safety at Sea.

The sea is, and always has been a dangerous place and a fisherman's job is said to be the most dangerous in the World. On the afternoon of 18th August 1848, the weather was favourable on the Moray Firth and from Wick to Stonehaven around 800 boats left the many ports to go herring fishing. By midnight, the weather had deteriorated badly with gale force winds and heavy seas. During the storm, 124 fishing boats were lost, and 100 fishermen died, leaving behind 47 widows and 161 fatherless bairns, making this one of the worst maritime disasters on the east coast of Scotland. The disaster was considered so bad that the Government appointed Captain John Washington of the Admiralty to conduct an inquiry into it and to make recommendations for safety improvements in the fishing industry. Washington concluded that the open-decked design of the fishing boats was deficient, leaving the boats susceptible to swamping in heavy seas, and that many of the Moray Firth harbours were of poor quality and not inaccessible at all tidal conditions. In 1849, his report, entitled *'Report on the loss of life, and damage caused to fishing boats on the East Coast of Scotland, in the gale of 19th August 1848'* was presented to the House of Commons.

Most of the old photographs of steam drifters show a lifebuoy on the wheelhouse. Quite how useful this would be in a raging sea is debatable, nevertheless at the beginning of the 20th century safety was becoming more important, but advances in navigation equipment were still some way off. Prior to this, in the days of sail, fishermen stayed within sight of the shore, but the quest to catch more meant sailing further afield, and the introduction of the steam drifter realised this dream. Bigger steam driven boats were capable of sailing much further to catch fish, no matter the wind.

Much has been said about the fishermans sixth sense when it came to navigation, but how can this possibly work, and yet somehow in the days before the compass, fishermen somehow found their way around the vast space that is the sea, whilst it's true to say the night sky with its wealth of stars was useful this didn't really happen that often, more often the stars would be obscured by poor weather and so maybe there was such a thing as a sixth sense.

Macduff Harbour Barometer.
The Macduff Harbour Barometer can be seen inside Macduff Fish Market. It was donated to Macduff by John Murray Esq. of London in 1849, one year after the 1848 disaster. The barometer was made by Adie & Son of Edinburgh. This barometer was originally located on the gable wall of a house in Shore Street, but was moved inside the new fish market when it was built in 1966.

Macduff Harbour Barometer. (S. Bruce).

By the mid 1850's the government of the time recognised that it was not only the boats and the harbours that needed improvements in safety, the weather also needed to be considered. The Government decided that each port should have a barometer so the skippers could be aware of possible changes in the weather. Prior to this, fishing boats set sail with no idea what the forthcoming weather could be, and often got caught out, with a resulting loss of life.

Robert Fitzroy. (Herman John Schmidt).

Vice-Admiral Robert Fitzroy (1805 to 1865) former Naval Hydrographer born in Suffolk believed that many ships and lives were lost at sea simply because the fishermen left port unaware of coming storms. In order to remedy this, he had a specially designed 'fishery barometer' issued to every port. Their large clear scales bear 'Fitzroy's Rules'. The ports that could not afford one got theirs free, others had to pay or have it paid for by local businesses. Fitzroy's barometers must have saved thousands of lives over the years.

Banff Harbour Barometer.

On the north wall of the former Banff Brewery building can be seen a box which once held the Banff Harbour Barometer, and adjacent to it a notice board. The whereabouts of the Banff barometer is unknown, although a local elderly gentleman reckons it was taken to Fraserburgh. The box and the notice board were in 2010 restored by the Banffshire Maritime & Heritage Association. Portgordon Harbour has a dummy barometer in their box, and the Banff box now has similar. The notice board now has information displayed regarding Banff Brewery, the Battery Green, the Barometer, and the Coastguard.

Banff Harbour Barometer Box and Notice Board, Battery Green, prior to refurbishment. (S. Bruce).

Barometer Box and Notice Board, Battery Green, Banff, after repairs. (S. Bruce).

Crew Members.

A typical crew of an early sailing drifter was 3 to 4 men, later larger sailing boats had 6 to 8 of a crew. A steam drifter crew comprised of eight to twelve men, but typically ten men as follows:

Skipper, mate, engineer/driver, cook, stoker (Fireman who looked after the boiler), and five deckhands.

There was no second engineer on drifters though there would have been on trawlers.

Shares in the Boat / Wages.

Typically, payment for the whole crew depended very much on the catch, though there was a difficult balancing act to consider. A good catch did not necessarily mean a good return, as a big catch, replicated by others in the fleet, could lead to a lower price as the fish were plentiful at market and so the price fell, on the other hand a small catch might well provide a decent return, again dependent on the market.

The crew got their wages after the running cost of the boat was paid, and the netmen were paid. The nets were typically owned by the skipper, mate, and the hired hands.

The bounty system whereby skippers contracted to curers in return for a fixed bounty worked reasonably well until about 1884, when an abundance of fish brought the price tumbling down ruining many a curer in the process. There followed some uncertain years, however the advent of the auction in 1887 brought about a better system for all, although there still remained the problem of too many fish bringing about a lower market price and a lower return for all concerned.

Provisions.

Onboard the crew would dine on salted beef and other preserved foods, which in the northeast included our much loved butteries. Herring was also eaten, usually fried in oatmeal. Local grocers and bakers benefitted greatly from supplying their goods to the fishing fleet. Worth mentioning, is that Macduff at one point in time had seven bakers.

World War 1.

When WW1 was declared (4th August 1914), hundreds of Banff and Macduff men enthusiastically enlisted in the forces, with many of the fishermen choosing to enlist with the Admiralty, where their knowledge of the sea was hugely appreciated. Virtually all of the local fishing boats were requisitioned by the Admiralty. The boats were used for minesweeping, tender, and patrol duties, and many of them had a gun fitted. 300, possibly 301 of the Banff and Macduff men died, and many received awards for bravery. 'Macduff Roll of Honour 1914 – 1919', ISBN 978-0-9547960-7-5 gives details of the awards for bravery, prisoners of war, and the losses of life, not just at sea, but encompassing all the services during the war. It was re-published in 2008 by the Banffshire Maritime & Heritage Association, and it has a story titled 'Taken Prisoner' based on an account by George McKay of Macduff.

Skipper George McKay and William John Watt, of BF662 'Helenora', holding a flag captured from an Austrian Pirate in the Adriatic during WW1.

World War 2.

With the outbreak of war (1ˢᵗ September 1939) the call was made to the fishing fleets for assistance, and as one can imagine there was little resistance to this, in fact quite the opposite. The fishermen remembered the part their forbearers had played in the 1914 to 1918 conflict and were quick to respond. Some who had served in the earlier conflict also served in this one. The Admiralty had seen the good work carried out by the fishermen during WW1, and were keen to use them in this latest fight for freedom and deployed their craft in a number of ways, minesweeping being a good example. Fishing boats were used as tenders and to deploy anti-submarine nets, with many having a gun fitted forward and a canvas lookout fitted above the wheelhouse. (See page 45 for an example). During the conflict, many fishing boats were lost, simply because these boats fitted with rudimentary armoury were easy prey for the German U-boats. However, this did not deter the brave fishermen, they certainly knew the meaning of fear, but they also knew where their duty lay, and many gave their lives for the cause. It is testimony to these men that their work was recognised so the nation will remember. The rather poignant book entitled 'Trawlers go to War' by Paul Lund and Harry Ludham ISBN 978-0450011757, is worth a read. Harry Tate's Navy gives a good insight into the wonderful work done by this section of society, which also included service on other small craft, they became known as the Royal Naval Patrol Service and there is a memorial to them at what was once their headquarters at Sparrows Nest, Lowestoft.

A very busy Shore Street, Macduff in the 1940's.

Banff Harbour Pre-1935. (Photographer unknown).

Herring Fishing in Banff.
Herring fishing, thanks to bounties offered by the British Government commenced in Banff circa 1816. The whole of the Moray Firth Coast was buzzing with the new opportunities the herring fishing was bringing, and local men were quick to take advantage of this newly found prosperity. At Banff, the Lighthouse Quay was built between 1818 and 1828 at a cost of £7,000 by civil engineer Thomas Telford (1757 to 1834); this extension increased the size of Banff Harbour to four acres, giving much more space for the rapidly increasing fleet. Things finally took off when Edinburgh born Walter Biggar (1787 to 1867) married local lass Ann Duff in 1821 and settled in Banff. By this time Banff had nearly seventy herring boats. The number of boats in Banff peaked at ninety in 1822. Walter Biggar is recognised as being the man who established links to sell herring with the Baltic countries, and he and his wife are commemorated by the Biggar Fountain, which was erected in 1878, and proudly stands in Low Street, Banff. The fountain was gifted by the Rev. Dr. and Mrs. Blaikie who were relatives of the Biggar's. It is said that they were inspired to make the gift after reading the life of Banff naturalist Thomas Edward (1814 to 1886), who had said that it would be an advantage to the town to have a memorial sited on the original site of Banff's Mercat Cross.

Biggar Fountain of 1878,
Low Street Banff. (S. Bruce).

Walter Biggar (1787 to 1867).
(Photographer unknown).

The following fish curer's had businesses in Banff; Messrs. Nesbit & Co. formerly Messrs. Walter Biggar & Co., and Messrs. Grant & Co. formerly Messrs. Grapel & Co. The house of Alexander Murray of Whitehills also transacted his business from Banff. See Appendix E for others.

Herring fishing was restricted in Banff due to the want of available space near the harbour for the establishment of curing yards, and due to the high rates of dues. Hence, the harbour at Macduff was better placed to take full advantage of the herring boom, and duly did so, becoming the commercial fishing centre, with Banff acting as the county town. Fishing boat registration became mandatory in 1839. The 'BF' boat registration for Banffshire begun in 1843, which included all ports from Portgordon to Fraserburgh. On the 1st April 1896, 'FR' for Fraserburgh was introduced, and this district included all the villages from Rosehearty to St. Combs. In 1907, 'BCK' for Buckie was also established independently of Banff.

The barrels of cured herring were shipped to the Baltic countries in British and Prussian ships. Prussian ships were favoured by many of the foreign buyers because they could be hired for a much lesser fee; however, the ships that did sail from Banff were 50 / 50 British and Prussian. Most of the British ships sailed to London for shipment to the West Indies; others sailed to Liverpool for shipment to Ireland. After the arrival of the railway to Banff Harbour Station in 1859 (Official opening date 31st March 1860) the cured herring was also transported south by train, the railway line is said to have run down to the pier immediately south of the Lighthouse Quay. Banff Harbour Railway Station closed to passengers 6th July 1964 and to freight in 1968.

Banff Harbour Railway Station c1950. (Photographer unknown).

The ships hired to transport the barrels of herring would return with cargoes of grain, wool, bark, iron, hemp, flax and hides; and of course, cargoes of larch and later fir wood from Norway, which was required to make the herring barrels. The town and harbour also hosted ancillary industries such as coal merchants, ship chandlers, rope, and sail-makers.

The following table for Banff is taken from The New Statistical Account of Scotland 1845.

No. off / Date.	1831	1832	1833	1834	1835
Barrels cured.	1759	1959	1265	938	631
Boats employed.	14	16	18	22	8
Fishermen.	56	64	72	88	32
Women curing & packing.	41	46	48	60	21
Coopers.	6	6	6	8	4
Curers.	5	5	5	6	4

The table shows a fluctuation in numbers, this is thought to be due to the herring fishing being poor in 1835. See Appendix E.

The Account also states with regard to the revenue of the Post Office "A very considerable portion of the revenue is derived from the correspondence with the northern parts of the continent, on account of the herring fishery".

Banff Harbour late 19ᵗʰ century. (Photographer unknown).
(Note the herring barrels on MacDonald's Jetty (East Quay), photo centre).

During the 1880's and 1890's sailboats became larger, this was mainly due to the invention of the Steam Capstan, which was affectionately referred to as the 'Iron Man'. A small steam engine turned the capstan, which was used to pull in the nets or hoist the sails. Since the steam capstan was much more powerful than the crew manhandling the nets and sails this enabled larger nets to be shot, thereby requiring larger boats to hold the catch, which in turn led to larger sails on the boats. MacDonald Brothers in nearby Portsoy were famous for manufacturing steam capstans – their patented capstan was said to be unique because it could also go in reverse.

FR958 'Reaper' steam capstan. (S. Bruce).

During the days of sail, the fishermen rowed in and out of the harbour when there was no wind. To make life easier for the fishermen in the late 19th century a steam powered paddle tug was used to tow the fishing boats in and out of the harbour. This tug is also known to have towed fishing boat hulls to Aberdeen to have their engines fitted.

Steam Paddle Tug in Banff Bay around 1900. (BM&HA Archive).

In the early 1900's sailboats were being replaced with steam drifters, and these were bigger boats with greater drafts. The wooden hulled drifters built in Banff ranged between 50 and 100 tons gross, seventy-five to ninety feet long, with a beam of around eighteen feet, and a depth of eight to ten feet. Banff Harbour was too small to accommodate all of these, and only had a maximum depth of twelve feet at high tide rising to fifteen feet during Spring tides. At low tide, the boats in Banff Harbour were high and dry. Due to Banff Harbour only being accessible during short periods of the tide and prone to silting, many fishermen began to berth across the bay in the much deeper, more accessible, and more spacious harbour of Macduff.

Because the boats were bigger and steam powered this meant that the fishermen could fish farther offshore and it was much easier for them to 'follow the herring' to other ports all around Great Britain. Herring are migratory and during the season could only be caught in certain locations. From May to August, they would travel from the Shetland Isles south to Leith. Then from September to November, they travelled down the English coast with the local fishermen following them as far as Yarmouth and Lowestoft. During January to March, herring could also be caught off the west coast. This 'following of the herring' meant that local fishermen spent months at a time away from home, landing their catch at a variety of ports. Many of the local girls referred to as 'Herring Lassies' or 'Gutting Quines' also 'followed the herring' travelling on ferries, trains, and sometimes on a drifter to get to the next port. The lassies worked in teams of three, with two gutting and one packing. Banff girls, some as young as fourteen, are known to have travelled as far north as Shetland, and as far south as Lowestoft 'following the herring.' On their travels many of the lassies lived in rather basic wooden huts supplied by the Curer, or if they were lucky in a guesthouse.

Fish market on the quay, Macduff.
(Courtesy S. Bruce, Peterhead).

Modern Pelagic Fishing Boats.

These huge boats can catch an enormous 1,400 tonnes of fish in one shot. Nowadays the fish mostly mackerel rather than herring are hoovered from the net into a tank of salt water and kept fresh, the fishermen don't even need to handle the fish or the nets. Once in port, the tank is discharged directly into the fish-processing factory.

Macduff Harbour lighthouse built 1903. (S. Bruce).

Length: 61.5m. Built: 2003.   IMO No. 9274795.
Breadth: 13m.
Draught: 7.2m.   Owners: Castlehill LLP, Fraserburgh.
GRT: 1731te.

BF50 'Resolute', Fraserburgh Harbour. (S. Bruce).

Length: 61.5m. Built: 2002. IMO No. 9256810.
Breadth: 13.2m.
Draught: 6m.
GRT: 1632te. Operated by Mewstead (Fraserburgh) LLP.

BF77 'Ocean Quest', Fraserburgh Harbour. (S. Bruce).

Length: 58m. Breadth: –12m. Draught: –7m. GRT: 1424te.

Built: 1997.

IMO No. 9147148.

BF70 'Krossfjord'. (S. Bruce).

Banff Harbour late 19th century. (BM&HA Archive)
(Note the herring barrels and the farlane on the pier).

In the foreground of the above photograph is a Morton patent slip which was erected here in 1836, it had the capacity to lift boats of up to 300 tons.

A very busy Banff Harbour pre1935. (BM&HA Archive).

During WW1 (1914 to 1918), the Admiralty requisitioned fishing boats for minesweeping, patrol boat, and tender duties, which they performed admirably. After the war, the market for herring in the Baltic countries collapsed and many of the curers were declared bankrupt. Herring fishing continued after WW1, but on a much smaller scale, with most of the Banff fishermen then concentrating on fishing for white fish, and most berthed in Macduff or other harbours. A little over a century after it began, 1920 is recorded as the last year herring was landed at Banff. Peter Anson wrote in 1930 that the harbour "Is now seldom used by fishing craft for landing their fish"; however he also wrote that "The harbour is often full of steam drifters between the various fishing seasons". "There are now seventeen steam drifters owned here". He also states that in 1929, no herring were landed at Banff and only £59 of white fish, this compared to £18,522 of white fish landed in Macduff shows the decline of Banff as a fishing port.

A packed Banff Harbour 1911. We can date this photo to 1912, since BF303 'Elegant' on the left with no wheelhouse was built at this date. BF1312 'Pansy' (centre) and BF257 'Productive' (Right). (Photographer unknown).

Banff Harbour 1928. (John D. McAree of Stirling).

Today we see Banff Harbour chiefly as a marina for pleasure craft. The harbour was subject to major works including deepening and fitting of pontoons during 2006, and officially opened as a marina in 21st April 2007.

Banff Herring Fishers.

In their wee sailing drifters,
They heid oot tae the sea,
The fishermen o' Banff,
Cast aff fae the Lighthouse Quay.

They're aff fishin' fer the herrin',
In their locally biggit boats,
The Banff herrin' fleet,
Took plenty chance shots.

During the summer months,
They'd cast oot their nets,
An' return tae Banff Hairber,
Tae fill their baskets.

In the hairber they'd unload the fish,
An' tak them tae the gutting lines,
Far they wir gutted an' sa'ated,
By the mony gutting quines.

Boat-building at Stevenson &
Asher, Banff Harbour, c1950.
(BM&HA Archive).

The herrin' they did cure,
An' they dried an' pickled the cod,
Packin' them intae barrels,
Tae send them far abroad.

Tae Australia an' Russia,
Mony ships fae Banff did sail,
Carryin' Scottish cured herrin',
An' aye, mony a letter or a packet, for the Royal Mail.

Stanley Bruce.

Banff Boat-builders.

There were two prominent boat-builders in Banff who built steam drifters, and these were W. & G. Stephen, Greenbanks, and Stevenson & Asher, Banff Harbour. These two companies built <u>at least</u> seventy-three Banff (BF) registered wooden hulled steam drifters or trawlers between 1906 and 1919; they also built many other boats for other ports. These two companies built the wooden hulls and deckhouses, but not the steam engines or boilers. Watson an engineering firm in Carmelite Street, was renowned for building and fitting steam engines on drifters, and would have installed many of them on the Banff built boats. At the end of WW1, the Admiralty had a surplus of steam drifters and they passed seventy-five boats to the Scottish Fishery Board. These were sold to fishermen at a price lower than the cost of building a new boat, and this had a drastic impact on boat-building activities in Banff. After WW1, the diesel engine took over from steam, with engines that were far more economical to run, and negated the need for a Stoker – giving one less wage to pay. W. & G. Stephen built at least sixty-tree steam drifters or trawlers, with at least fifty-one BF registered, and twelve others. Stevenson & Asher built at least twenty-two Banff registered steam drifters or trawlers. See Appendices A, and B for details.

'HMD Ray'. (Built by W. & G. Stephen, Banff, 1917).

In March 1905, Stevenson and Asher Boat-builders, Banff Harbour launched their first steam drifter, it was small by drifter standards at only 44 feet long, and was built for Portsoy owners.

c1935, the capstan and beacon pole were removed from the Lighthouse Quay at Banff Harbour and the lighthouse was erected. The capstan at the end of the lighthouse quay was prior to this used to pull the sailing drifters into the harbour.

Banff Harbour c1930.
(Photographer unknown).

Banff Harbour and light 2004.
(S. Bruce).

The wood for making herring barrels was imported from Scandinavia, and according to the Banff Fishery Officers record book 1871 to 1877, from 1871 to 1873 larch was used, and from 1874 to 1877 fir was used. Herring barrels are also known to have been made from Norwegian birch. The ships that exported the cured herring were the ships that returned with the timber, oak which was used for boatbuilding, and larch or fir for making herring barrels.

*Boatbuilding at Banff Harbour c1950, BF134 'Fairdawn' and 'Fairhaven'
under construction. (Frank Ritchie). (Note the gas works at the rear).*

Herring baskets, such as the one shown were used to lift the herring from the fishing boat to the quay. They were then taken often by horse to the farlanes to be gutted. Baskets were of a specific size and held 7 stone of herring. Each had two crown marks, see page 9 for an example.

A Typical Herring Basket. (S. Bruce).

Herring Fishing in Macduff.

Macduff located in Banffshire on the Moray Firth coast of Scotland has long been associated with fishing, and many have sought to record the life and times of the fishing industry in these parts, perhaps the most notable being marine artist and writer Peter F. Anson (1889 to 1975), who spent almost 20 years in Macduff. Peter's book titled 'Life on the Low Shore' published in 1969 gives many details of local interest.

Herring fishing was not the only fishing ongoing in Macduff – the fishermen caught white fish such as cod, haddock, etc., and on the River Deveron, and out in the bay fishermen caught salmon. At No. 7 Union Road, the derelict former salmon bothy (Category B listed) built early 19th century still stands today.

Former Salmon Bothy, No. 7 Union Road, Macduff. (S. Bruce).

The herring fishing industry relied on other industries and services such as, sail-makers, rope-works, sawmills, ship chandlers, fish salesmen, and boat-builders; and in Macduff itself seven bakers, butchers, and grocers, all flourished supplying the boats with their merchandise.

The Beginning.

At the end of the 17th century Macduff was a small cluster of houses known as Doune (Doun or Down, Dun in Gaelic means fort) situated in the Thanedome of Glendowachy, which prior to 1748[1] was ruled by the Earl of Buchan who was the Hereditary Sheriff of Banffshire.

1) Hereditary sheriffdoms were abolished after Culloden (1746), in an Act dated 1748.

The village gradually grew over the years, and it was towards the end of the eighteenth century under its then owner James Duff (1729 to 1809) 2nd Earl Fife, that fishing was formally established in a small but enthusiastic way. Until that time, the men of Doune and many other ports went to sea in small open-decked boats, and caught fish, but that was simply to benefit the local lairds, and to place food on the family table, with seemingly no real thought for the future. Early in the 19th century, fishing was considered somewhat haphazard, with the lairds seemingly uninterested in the fishermen's welfare, and perhaps only looking for financial gain. Parliament took notice and brought about legislation to improve the lot of the fisher folk and in so doing gained support from the people they were helping. From 1808 to 1821 there were six Parliamentary Acts passed concerning herring fishing. Parliament had, it seemed, recognised the growing value and immense potential of the fishing industry to not just local economies but also to the wealth of the nation, and during the 18th to 20th century issued a raft of legislation (See Appendix D). Fishing was to become vital to the economic growth of the nation. Those with foresight to see this certainly contributed to history.

Why Macduff?

With its deepwater harbour, Macduff was ideally situated along a rugged coastline that not only gave good access to the Moray Firth but also eastward to the North Sea with its rich fishing grounds. Macduff Harbour could accommodate deeper drafted cargo vessels than Banff, which was so important in the export of herring. In addition, the coming of the railway 4th June 1860 meant that barrels of cured herring could be transported further and faster than ever before, sometimes arriving as far as London the same day they were landed.

Macduff Harbour.

Macduff Harbour was first established in 1770, when the East and West Harbours were built.

Macduff Harbour in 1830.

In 1830, Lord Fife's Breakwater was built.

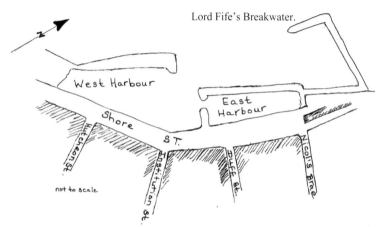

Macduff Harbour 1830. (Drawing by Kay Smith).

Macduff Harbour in 1878.

In 1878, the North Basin was built.

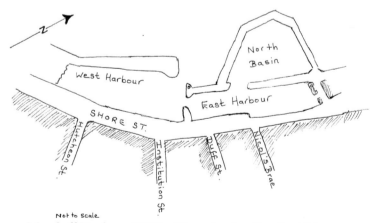

Macduff Harbour 1878. (Drawing by Kay Smith).

Macduff Harbour in 1921.
The slipway and the Princess Royal Basin were built.

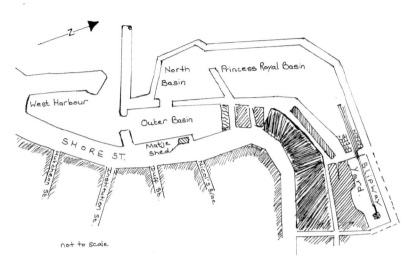

Macduff Harbour 1921. (Drawing by Kay Smith).

Macduff Harbour in 1966. (Much as it is today).

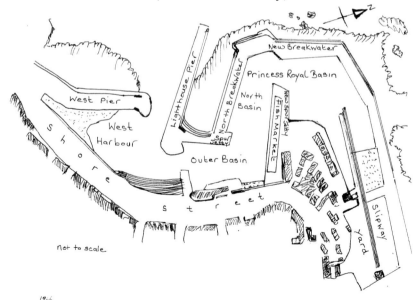

Macduff Harbour 1966. (Drawing by Kay Smith).

Today's view of Macduff Harbour is very different from that of earlier years.

Macduff Harbour and anchor, as viewed from the Town Cross. (S. Bruce).

A packed Macduff Harbour late 19ᵗʰ century. (BM&HA Archive).

Macduff Harbour Key Dates.

1698	The Convention of Royal Burghs authorised the grant of 500 merks to Banff 'towards the building of a new pier at the town of Downe, which they are to purchase'. However, nothing came of this.
1732	The village of Downe is recorded as consisting of only a few fisher houses.
1733	William Duff (1697 to 1763) of Braco (Lord Braco from 1735 and 1st Earl Fife from 1759) bought the lands of Doune.
1747-55	Roy's map of this date shows no buildings where the harbour now stands.
1770	The East and West Harbours were built by James Duff 2nd Earl Fife.
1783	Downe was renamed Macduff.
1815	The first yard for curing herring was established in Macduff.
1820 to 1830	Lord Fife's breakwater was built. Lord Fife being James Duff (**1776** to **1857**) the 4th Earl Fife.
c1830	A fierce storm destroyed 150 feet of Lord Fife's Breakwater.
1847	2nd July - The Macduff Harbour Act was passed. This authorised the Trustees to improve and extend the harbour, and to charge fees.
1878	The North Basin was built. It was officially opened by Mr. Tayler, Commissioner to Viscount Macduff.
1898	Ownership of Macduff Harbour was transferred from the Duff family to Macduff Town Council.
1903	The Lighthouse Quay was built.
1914	4th August - WW1 was declared, and during the war, the Admiralty requisitioned almost all of Macduff's forty steam drifters and trawlers.
1921	25th May - The Princess Royal officially opened the slipway and the Princess Royal Basin.
1939-45	Most of the BF registered boats were requisitioned by the Admiralty. Boats for the Admiralty were built in Macduff.
1949-52	The Princess Royal Basin & North Basin were deepened to at least 8 feet at low water Spring tide & a jetty was removed.

1955	December – On the site where the 'Matje Shed' stood at the harbour, a new building was opened, which accommodated the fish market, the Harbour Master's office, HM Customs and Excise, the Fishery Officer, and the Coastal Fish Selling Company. These offices remained until 1983.
1966	The old Fish Market was demolished and a new fish market built. Peter Anson's former cottage Harbourhead was demolished.
2008-9	The new slipway was built.

Macduff Harbour 1903, BF1206 'Heather Belle' Zulu sailing herring drifter.

In the centre of the above picture, a small train can be seen. In January 1903 this train and sections of railway track bought by Macduff Harbour Board for circa £650 arrived at Macduff. The train was used to transport excavated materials from the harbour during the building of the Lighthouse Quay and associated harbour excavation work. The excavated materials were dumped on the beach at the west end of Union Road (Roughly where the filling station currently stands). During December 1903, the traction engine and the locomotive were stored at the Salmon Close under a partly covered wooden shed. The train and associated equipment was put up for sale in 1905.

Macduff Harbour benefited due of the introduction of the larger steam drifters, because fishermen from Banff, Pennan, Crovie, and Gardenstown had to move from their small more tidal harbours to the deeper and more spacious harbour of Macduff.

Following the building of the east and west basins of Doune Harbour in 1770, more fisher folk were attracted to the area to take advantage of the new facilities and they were eventually able to use the harbour at almost any tidal state. This meant no more waiting for the right tide to enter or leave and soon this improvement meant that the economies of fishing could be better exploited. The faster turnaround added greatly to the profitability of the fleet. Not only did they begin to see a better life, although still a dangerous one, the fishermen and the local economy thrived. The northeast was fast becoming part of a massive industry and a considerable source of income for the government of Great Britain.

From 1820 to 1830, Lord Fife's 400 feet long breakwater was built. It was funded by James Duff (**1776** to **1857**) the 4th Earl Fife. 150 feet of the northern end of the breakwater was destroyed by storms c1830. Once the storms abated, the stone blocks were left roughly in a line 90º to the breakwaters original location. This new line of stones was in 1878 used as the foundations for the North Basin harbour wall.

The Fishermans Attire.
Fishermen were easily recognised by their attire. (See photo page 43).
Knitted gansey – knitted by their wives or other family members to different patterns.
Knitted socks.
Bonnet.
Oilskins.

BF859. (Photographer unknown)

Fisheries Board.

Herring fishing was strictly controlled by the government, (See Appendix D), and a fishery officer was stationed at Banff (Later in Macduff). He kept records of fishing activities in the district, and his records for 1871 to 1877 included the following:

1) Number of fishermen and boys; number off, tonnage and value of fishing boats.
2) Number of boats and value of fishing nets.
3) Number of Coopers, gutting quines, carters, labourers, fish curers and those gathering bait and baiting lines.
4) Tonnage of boats importing salt and wood for barrel making, and those exporting herring and other white fish.
5) Amount of fresh herring sold.
6) Names of fish curers and number of barrels made.

Banff District Fishery Officer's leather note book 1871 to 1877. (Courtesy Buckie and District Fishing Heritage).

See Appendix E for further information.

Macduff Ice Factory.

Ice had been used by local salmon fishermen since the 18th century; it was collected in the winter and stored in an ice house. The salmon bothy No. 7 Union Road had such a facility. The herring did not need ice because they were pickled in brine, however the white fish did, and Macduff had its own ice factory, which made ice and supplied it to the local fishermen. This factory was demolished in 2007, and today Macduff Ship Design offices stand on this site.

On the left – the former Macduff Ice Factory prior to demolition. (S. Bruce).

Boat-building.

Names synonymous with boatbuilding in Macduff are Duncan, Slater, George Innes and Sons, Paterson, and Watt.

The 'Heather Sprig' BCK181 built in 1997 was the first boat built in Macduff with a steel hull; all locally built boats prior to this date were built with wooden hulls.

Macduff.

William Duff of Braco (Later 1st Earl Fife) bought the village of Doune around 1732, which at the time "Consisted of no more than a few fisher houses". In 1783, his son and heir James Duff 2nd Earl Fife received a charter from King George II renaming the village Macduff, and constituting it as a burgh. In honour of the occasion he rebuilt the market cross adjacent to the parish church, part of which is said to come from the county of Fife.

The harbour, safer and more accessible than that of, Banff, was constructed by the Earls Fife from 1770 to 1878; and transferred to the burgh in 1898.

25th May 1921 – The Princess Royal Basin was officially opened by Princess Louise (1867 to 1931) HRH the Princess Royal and her daughter Princess Maud. The new basin nearly doubled the area of the harbour to a little over six acres.

The decline in the herring industry has been attributed to a number of factors; over-fishing certainly reduced stocks, there is no doubt with more foreign registered boats attracted to the fishing grounds, their presence accelerated matters, and export levels began to fall. At home, people's diets were changing; with increases in farming production food was becoming more available and cheaper giving people more choice, with many no longer choosing herring

It was simply not sustainable to have such a large fishing fleet, and with the lack of conservation control, it was easy to see, perhaps with hindsight how the industry began to falter and eventually reduce to a scale only a fraction of its former self in its heyday.

BF396 Herring Sailboat.
(Photographer unknown).

Macduff Harbour Today.

Today's view of Macduff Harbour shows the harbour area as home to a number of fishing boats, occasional visits by cargo boats and the site of a shipbuilding yard that has progressed through many difficult times, and yet continues to flourish providing much needed local jobs and hope for the future. Whilst some fish are still unloaded at Macduff, most of them are quickly taken elsewhere for processing.

The 'Puffin' a small converted fishing boat takes visitors on leisurely trips along the coast, more often seeking wildlife other than fish.

Puffin in Banff Bay. (S. Bruce).

Ship-repair at Macduff.

With so many boats fishing out of Macduff, the ship-repair business was kept busy.

In 1922, a slipway was built by the Town Council on reclaimed ground at Bankhead at the east end of the harbour. The ground was reclaimed using the excavations from the Princess Royal Basin, which officially opened 25th May 1921. Prior to this, this area was used by Duncan Boat-builders who built Zulu sailboats.

During WW2, several Macduff drifters were requisitioned by the Admiralty for minesweeping and patrol duties, and on the slip at Macduff, several wooden hulled minesweepers were built.

August 2008, at a cost of £3.9 million a new safer modernised slip was opened at Macduff Harbour – this slip can take larger and beamier boats; however, the number of boats accommodated by the slip was reduced from seven to four.

Herring Curing in Macduff.
The first yard for herring curing was established in Macduff in 1815. During the subsequent 'Herring Boom', twelve curing yards were established in the town. As can be seen from the photograph below, it was not difficult establishing a curing yard; all that was needed was a decent sized piece of land to make and store barrels, and a wooden farlane to hold the herring to be gutted. You can also see from the photograph that the women gutters had no protection from the elements; this was the case in most of the yards. See Appendix E.

Fishermen had 24 hours to get the herring to shore, after that they began to deteriorate and became less valuable, the gutting quines would work until the catch was processed, often into the small hours.

Women gutting herring, at the farlane, Macduff, c1910.

According to the New Statistical Account of Scotland 1845, in 1836/7 Macduff exported 8,173 barrels of herring. The processing of the herring would have been carried out during the herring season, which locally was from June to September.

Getting ready for sea with freshly painted floats, Macduff Harbour 1928.
(John D. McAree of Stirling).

Danish Seine Net.

In 1920, the Government removed guaranteed prices for herring and prices dropped dramatically. Some fishermen had noticed that the Danish fishermen using the Seine Net were landing large quantities of white fish, and in the early 1920's some of the fishermen of Macduff adopted this method of fishing for white fish instead of fishing for herring.

This method involved the net shot, and resting just below the water surface with the boat turning a wide circle. Once the end of the net is picked-up, the bottom of the net is drawn in with a purse line. This prevents the fish escaping, and was certainly very productive.

These simple explanations of the type of method used to catch fish are helpful in demonstrating how productivity evolved but they are nothing without the skill of the fisherman. After all, the Skipper has to find the fish before they can be caught, and there lies a skill in itself. Fish do not simply appear, they have to be found. The early fishermen had none of the modern day electronic aids such as sonar and radar or even radio to help them. Even more reason to wonder at their unique ability to seek what cannot be seen, and find what cannot be found. No wonder we wonder at their enterprise.

Herring in Gamrie Bay.
The Banffshire Journal in August 1956 reported as follows:
"It was reported that for the first time in 20 years, a shoal of herring swam into Gamrie Bay, and from Wednesday until Friday of that week boats of every shape and description were leaving the harbour to take part in this unusual silver harvest. Their presence was first discovered, literally right on the doorstep of Crovie houses, by Mr. James Watt, No. 43, Crovie, who was fishing only a few yards from the shore at the village with a seine net in an effort to catch some saithe to use as bait for his lobster pots. When pulling up the net Mr. Watt found that it was unusually heavy. It had good reason to be for, instead of the few saithe that he had expected, it held nearly four boxes of herring. The following evening two other Crovie men, Mr. John Watt, No. 53, and another, Mr. John Watt of No. 64, went out to try their luck and were

successful. These successes acted as a signal to every other boat in the vicinity to have a go and on Thursday and Friday mornings of that week Gamrie Bay was full of small boats. One possible reason for the shoal was that during a recent gale the sea bottom had been stirred up and the regular feeding grounds of the fish may have been broken up, making it necessary for them to find food nearer the shore."

The Last Steam Drifter.
It seems appropriate to end with information on the last steam drifter built in Scotland and perhaps the UK. The last Steam Drifter built was the 'Wilson Line' built in Aberdeen by Alexander Hall & Co. in 1932 as yard No. 638 for William C. Wilson, Whitley Bay, as the 'Wilson Line' registered in Kirkcaldy KY322.
Official Number: 131884.
123 GRT, 52 tons Net, 94.25 feet long x 19.7 feet depth x 10.5 feet beam.
Hull – steel. Engine: 36 HP triple cylinder.
Last seen in Greece in the 1980's.

KY322 'Wilson Line', Aberdeen Harbour. (Photographer unknown).

Steam Drifters BF336 'Milky Way' and BF922 'Blossom' in Macduff Harbour 1928. (John D. McAree of Stirling).

Mizzen Sails.

These sails fitted to the stern of the boat were used to help steady the boat when the nets were out. As you can see from the pictures the style of the sail differed on a drifter to that on a trawler.

Drifter mizzen.   *Trawler mizzen.*

Cooking Herring.

The majority of the herring caught was gutted, salted, and packed in barrels within 24 hours. However, herring that were sold locally were often filleted and cooked fresh e.g. fried in oatmeal.

The salt-herring when removed from the barrel had to be steeped in a pot overnight, and then taken to the boil and the water changed a couple of times in order to reduce the saltiness.

Herring was, and still is sweet cured (pickled) in liquids such as conventional vinegar, but also nowadays marinated in such liquids as sherry, Madeira wine, cherry wine, or flavoured with herbs or berries. Orkney Herring Co. Ltd. has some particularly fine herring products.

Definitions.

Cran   Equals four baskets, and each basket held approximately 7 stone, which makes a cran 28 stone (178Kg).

Gansey   A knitted jumper.

Mizzen   A sail fitted to the aft mast, which was used to help steady the boat when its nets were out.

Pelagic   Of, relating to, or living in open oceans or seas, rather than waters adjacent to land or inland waters.

Shot   To cast the net.

White fish Cod, haddock, plaice etc.

References.

The New Statistical Account of Scotland, 1845.

Scottish Fisheries by James Thomson, 1849.

Fishing boats and fisher folk on the east coast of Scotland by Peter Anson, 1930.

Steam Drifters Recalled - Whitehills to St. Combs by Joseph Reid, 2001.

The Bard of Banff by Stanley Bruce 2004, ISBN 0-9547960-0-4.

The Herring Lassies – Following the Herring by Rosemary Sanderson 2008, ISBN 978-0-9547960-6-8.

Acknowledgements.

Whilst this book pays tribute to the fisher folk of the day, the fishermen and their hard working wives, it could not have been completed without the assistance of Macduff born James Gatt, himself a former fisherman, and his remarkable memory for detail which proved to be of great assistance.

Robert Andrew, Aberchirder for the use of his paintings (2 off).

Alex Tomlinson for his drawing of a herring.

Elizabeth Young (Nee McAree) for providing us with photographs taken by John D. McAree of Stirling (Her father).

Kay Smith, Banff for her various drawings.

Buckie and District Fishing Heritage, for the loan of the Banff Fishery Officers record book for 1871 to 1877.

◆ Herring Fishing - Banff and Macduff ◆

The following tables were put together from scratch, we did not have any boat-builders lists to work with, so we have added all the steam drifters we could find, but cannot guarantee these as complete lists.

APPENDIX A
Banff (BF) Registered Steam Drifters built by W. & G. Stephen Banff. (51, plus 1 conversion*).

No	Name	Date	Owners	Remarks
BF39	Budding Rose	1914	Henry Milne, Whitehills, & others.	Scrapped 1936
BF45	Craigalvah	1909	Alexander Paterson & A. J. Paterson, Macduff.	Scrapped 1951
BF59	Brighter Hope	1909	George Slater, Banff.	Scrapped 1937
BF61	Gilt Edge	1916	John Wood, Portknockie, & others.	Scrapped 1950
BF82	Deveronside	1914	Alexander Paterson, & W. Paterson, Macduff.	Scrapped 1946
BF85	Montcoffer	1909	George Anderson, Alex Paterson, & others Macduff.	Scrapped 1936
BF92	Gavenwood	1914	Alexander Paterson, & A. Wood, Macduff, & others.	Mined 1916
BF96	Kilnburn	1914	John James George, David McCallum, & A. McCallum, Macduff.	Scrapped 1936
BF103	Token	1914	W. S. Falconer, & Alex Paterson, Macduff.	Wrecked 1941 (WW2)
BF115	Gamrie Bay	1914	George West, J. West, G. West, Gardenstown, & others.	Scrapped 1950
BF122	Cullykhan	1910	George West & Co., Gardenstown.	Scrapped 1934
BF144	Gavenybrae	1910	Alex Wood (Park) Banff, James Wood, George & William Watson.	Scrapped 1935
BF169	Convallaria	1910	James Ritchie Gardenstown, & others.	Wrecked 1924
BF175	Dunedin	1910	Alex Paterson, J. W. Lovie, Macduff, & others.	Scrapped 1949
BF193	Gowanbank	1910	James Johnston, Gardenstown, & others.	Scrapped 1938
BF205	Wheat Stalk	1910	Jas. S. McGillvray, & William McGillvray, Macduff.	Scrapped 1952

APPENDIX A (continued)
Banff (BF) Registered Steam Drifters built by W. & G. Stephen Banff.
(51 plus 1 conversion*).

No	Name	Date	Owners	Remarks
BF247	Prospective	1910	J. Slater, Banff, G. Wood, & J. Wood, Sandend.	Scrapped 1938
BF271	White Daisy	1910	James Lovie (Scott), Gardenstown, & others.	Wrecked 1940 (WW2)
BF286	Ivy Leaf / Restore	1911	George West, William Chalmers Gardenstown, & others.	Scrapped 1949
BF303	Elegant	1911	John Wilson senior, & John Wilson junior, Banff, & others.	Scrapped 1936
BF330	Tea Rose	1911	G. Craigen, F. Nicol, Gardenstown, & others.	Scrapped 1945
BF345	Lily Bank / Braes o' Gamrie	1911	Alexander Brodie, Banff; J. Watt, Gardenstown, & others.	Scrapped 1937
BF350	Girl Evelyn	1911	John Wood Snr., Banff, & others.	Scrapped 1936
BF353	Silverford	1911	Alexander Barlow, Banff.	Wrecked 1921
BF393	Daisy Bank	1911	A. W. Thomson, Buckie, J. Hepburn, Gardenstown, & others.	Wrecked 1949
BF395	Uniflorous / Flowing Stream	1911	A. W. Thomson, Buckie, W. Cormack, Banff, & others.	Scrapped 1938
BF397	Coronaria	1911	William Kidd, J. Watt, Gardenstown, & others	Wrecked 1929
BF412	Refraction	1919	Built as HMD Refraction for the Admiralty – BF registered in 1920.	Scrapped 1954
BF428	Perila	1912	Alexander Watt, Gardenstown, & others.	Wrecked 1930
BF434	Speedwell IV	1906	W. Blackhall Snr., Gardenstown, & others.	Wrecked 1910
BF440	Rime	1919	Built as 'HMD Rime' for the Admiralty – BF registered in 1920.	Scrapped 1947
BF445	Lilacina	1912	Alex. Ritchie & Co., Gardenstown.	Scrapped 1938
BF465	Courage	1912	Alex. Paterson, T. C. Gordon, G. L. Thomson, Macduff, & others.	Scrapped 1938
BF528	Condor	1907	Alex Paterson, William Paterson, Macduff, & others.	Wrecked 1932

APPENDIX A (continued)
Banff (BF) Registered Steam Drifters built by W. & G. Stephen Banff.
(51 plus 1 conversion*). Continued.

No	Name	Date	Owners	Remarks
BF536	Forethought	1913	James Anderson, A.P. Robertson, James Watt, Crovie, George Walker Ltd., Fraserburgh, & George Craigen, Gardenstown.	Wrecked 1921
BF544	George A. West	1913	George A. West & Co., Macduff.	Wrecked 1927
BF545	British Crown	1913	Alexander Paterson & Co., Macduff.	Scrapped 1949
BF600	Ocean Gleaner	1913	A. Watt, Alex Johnston, G. Craigen, Gardenstown, & others.	Scrapped 1949
BF611	Jasper	1907	George West, John West, & James West, Gardenstown.	Scrapped 1939
BF614	Golden Feather	1913	William Blackhall Snr., Gardenstown, & others.	Wrecked 1922
BF615	Concordia	1913	A.W. Paterson, Macduff, & others.	Scrapped 1946
BF620	Thermopylae	1913	William West, & George West, Macduff.	Scrapped 1950
BF652	Lavatera	1913	John Wood Snr., Banff, & others.	Scrapped 1948
BF679	Fern	1907	Alexander Watt, G. Watt, Gardenstown, & others.	Scrapped 1949
BF687	Livelihood	1907	William Murray, Gardenstown.	Scrapped 1934
BF905	Lufra	1907	A. Wilson, & Alex Paterson, Macduff.	Scrapped 1932
BF1136	Gellyburn	1908	Alexander Paterson, Macduff, & others	Scrapped 1947
BF1145	Tarlair	1908	John J. George, & G. Watt, Macduff.	Scrapped 1936
BF1212* (Engine fitted 1909).	Water Lily	1899	J. Mair, Macduff, & others.	Scrapped 1924
BF1411	Norseman	1903	J. J. George Macduff, & others.	Wrecked 1912

APPENDIX B
Banff (BF) Registered Steam Drifters built by Stevenson & Asher, Banff. (22 off).

No	Name	Date	Owners	Remarks
BF57	Astrum Spei	1914	Alexander Watt, Banff, & others.	Sank 1916 (WW2).
BF81	Forglen	1909	James Falconer, Banff, & others.	Scrapped 1938
BF93	Craigneen	1914	James Ritchie, W. Ritchie, & J. Ritchie, Whitehills.	Wrecked 1940
BF136	Montbletton	1910	Alexander Wood, Banff, & others.	Scrapped 1938
BF149	Fragrance	1910	James (Jock) Wood, & Sons, Banff.	Scrapped 1936
BF195	Lustring	1910	James Wilson Snr., J. Wilson Jnr., & D. Wilson, Banff.	Wrecked 1918
BF231	Boyndie Burn	1910	William Slater, & J. Slater, Banff.	Scrapped 1948
BF257	Productive	1906	John Wood Snr., Banff, & others.	Sold 1923
BF260	Lily	1906	Henry Milne Jnr., Whitehills, & others.	Scrapped 1936
BF323	Clover	1911	Alexander Paterson, Macduff, & others.	Scrapped 1932
BF325	Cinceria	1911	William Sivewright, Banff, & others.	Wrecked 1920
BF326	Pressing On	1911	David Falconer, & R. Falconer, Banff.	Wrecked 1912
BF327	Silver Pearl	1911	George Mair, Banff, & others.	Scrapped 1948
BF364	Ruby Gem	1911	W. Wood, F. Wood, & A. Wood, Banff.	Lost to fire 1924
BF365	Barley Stalk	1917	James S. McGillivray, Macduff.	Scrapped 1939
BF394	Royal Burgh / John Robert	1911	Robert Watt, Henry Munro, Banff, & others.	Scrapped 1938
BF508	Proficiency	1913	David Falconer, & R. Falconer, Banff.	Scrapped 1938
BF526	Lustre Gem	1907	William Wilson, John Wilson, & Jas. Wilson, Banff.	Wrecked 1924
BF662	Helenora	1914	John Slater, & Helen Slater, Banff.	Sank 1917 (WW2)

APPENDIX B (continued)
Banff (BF) Registered Steam Drifters built by Stevenson & Asher, Banff. (22 off).

BF922	Blossom	1907	A. Paterson, J. Watt, Macduff, & others.	Scrapped 1934
BF968	Viola	1907	George West Snr., J. West, Gardenstown, & others.	Scrapped 1936
BF1140	The Colonel	1908	John J. George, Macduff, & others.	Scrapped 1947

APPENDIX C
Banff (BF) Registered Steam Drifters built by George Innes & Sons, Macduff. (11 off).

No	Name	Date	Owners	Remarks
BF75	Sprig of Heather	1914	Alexander Slater, Banff, & others.	Scrapped 1948.
BF77	Rosieburn	1909	Arthur Smith, Banff.	Broken up at Banff 1950.
BF108	Rose o' Doune	1910	F. J. Anderson, & William Paterson, Macduff.	Scrapped 1948.
BF253	Cedar Leaf	1910	Charles Thomson Snr., Macduff, & others.	Scrapped 1938.
BF301	Lonicera	1911	John McKay, Macduff, & others.	Wrecked 1925.
BF309	Corn Stalk	1916	Jas. S. McGillivray, Macduff.	Wrecked 1937.
BF311	Avondale	1911	W. Lyall, Walter Gerrard, Macduff, & others.	Sunk 15/5/17 during WW1.
BF359	John Watt	1911	John Watt, J. J. George, and others, Macduff.	Sunk in a collision 1921.
BF407	Look Sharp	1912	Alexander Paterson, Jas. Watt, & others, Macduff.	Scrapped 1932.
BF530	Replenish	1913	J. Mair, Macduff, & others.	Sunk in a collision 1931.
BF568	Vigorous	1913	George Slater, Alexander Paterson, Macduff, & others.	Scrapped 1939.

George Innes & Sons, Macduff also built steam drifters for other ports. The company also had a boat-building yard in Portknockie.
All of the above boats had wooden hulls; other BF registered boats built in Aberdeen were all built with steel hulls.

APPENDIX D
Herring Fishing Legislation – Acts of Parliament 1749 to 2009.

Date	Act
1749	Herring Fishery Act.
1753	Herring Fishery Act.
1755	Herring Fishery Act.
1757	Herring Fishery Act.
1765	Herring Fishery Act.
1771	White Herring Fisheries Act.
1772	Herring Fishery Act.
1779	White Herring Fishery Act.
1808	Herring Fishery (Scotland) Act.
1811	British White Herring Fishery Act.
1812	British White Herring Fishery Act.
1814	British White Herring Fishery Act.
1815	Herring Fishery (Scotland) Act.
1821	White Herring Fishery (Scotland) Act.
1851	Herring Fishery Act.
1858	Herring Fisheries (Scotland) Act.
1860	Herring Fisheries (Scotland) Act.
1861	White Herring Fishery (Scotland) Act.
1865	Herring Fisheries (Scotland) Act.
1867	Herring Fisheries (Scotland) Act.
1874	Herring Fishery Barrels Act.
1889	Herring Fisheries (Scotland) Act.
1890	Herring Fisheries (Scotland) Act, Amendment Act.
1895	Sea Fisheries Regulation (Scotland) Act.
1907	Sea Fisheries (Scotland) Application of Penalties.
1909	Trawling in Prohibited Areas prevention Act.
1913	Herring Fishery (Branding) Act.
1935	Herring Industry Act.
1938	Herring Industry Act.
1944	Herring Industry Act.
1948	White Fish & Herring Industries Act.
1953	White Fish & Herring Industries Act.
1957	White Fish & Herring Industries Act.
1964	Fishery Limits Act.

Date	Act
1968	Sea Fisheries Act.
1976	Fishery Limits Act.
1981	Fisheries Act.
1993	The Herring (Specified Sea Areas)(Prohibition of Fishing) Order.
1998	The Herring (Specified Sea Areas)(Prohibition of Fishing) Order.
2008	The Sea Fishing (Control Procedures for Herring, Mackerel and Horse Mackerel) (Scotland) Order.
2008	The Sea Fishing (Control Procedures for Herring, Mackerel and Horse Mackerel) (Scotland) Amendment Order.
2009	The Sea Fishing (Control Procedures for Herring, Mackerel and Horse Mackerel) (Scotland) Order.

You can clearly see from the above table that herring fishing was, and still is, one of the most legislated industries in the country.

The 1771 Act starts with a statement *"An Act for the Encouragement of the White Herring Fishery"*, how days have changed, our fishermen today are more likely to be discouraged to fish our seas.

BF1140 'The Colonel' built by Stevenson & Asher, Banff in 1908.
(Thought to have been scrapped c1947).

APPENDIX E
Herring Fishing Records for Banff District 1871 to 1877.

Table 1 - 1871 to 1877 - Number of Gutters and Packers.

Year	Crovie	Gardenstown	Macduff	Banff	Whitehills	Portsoy	Sandend	Total
1871	10	185	170	20	160	160	10	715
1872	10	215	180	20	160	160	10	755
1873	10	240	250	25	140	160	7	832
1874	6	270	303	40	120	160	6	905
1875	30	203	250	80	60	180	10	813
1876	20	200	200	80	60	180	0	740
1877	20	210	180	40	45	160	0	655

Table 2 - 1871 to 1877 - Number of Coopers.

Year	Crovie	Gardenstown	Macduff	Banff	Whitehills	Portsoy	Sandend	Total
1871	2	21	12	3	8	9	0	55
1872	2	21	16	4	8	10	0	61
1873	0	3	29	4	8	12	0	56
1874	1	30	36	6	8	10	0	91
1875	0	31	30	7	7	12	0	87
1876	0	22	20	12	8	8	0	70
1877	1	28	18	8	5	16	0	76

APPENDIX E (continued)
Herring Fishing Records for Banff District 1871 to 1877.

Table 3 - 1871 to 1877 - Number of Fishermen and Boys.

Year	Crovie	Gardenstown	Macduff	Banff	Whitehills	Portsoy	Sandend	Total
1871	240	230	220	90	190	120	80	1170
1872	230	220	200	116	180	120	82	1148
1873	210	220	210	120	170	128	86	1144
1874	230	266	254	116	205	150	100	1321
1875	230	252	244	106	195	150	90	1267
1876	220	230	220	130	190	150	100	1240
1877	200	260	240	130	190	150	100	1270

Table 4 - 1871 to 1877 - Number of Boats.

Year	Crovie	Gardenstown	Macduff	Banff	Whitehills	Portsoy	Sandend	Total
1871	69	81	99	29	80	40	29	427
1872	70	81	110	29	83	40	29	442
1873	66	68	112	33	83	46	27	435
1874	57	91	109	32	81	44	29	443
1875	63	90	109	35	83	40	26	446
1876	60	94	107	41	84	41	30	457
1877	59	95	110	41	84	44	30	463

APPENDIX E (continued)
Herring Fishing Records for Banff District 1871 to 1877.
Table 5 – Local Fish Curers.

Gardenstown	Macduff	Whitehills
John Fordyce & Co.	Andrew Wilson.	John Watson.
William Wiseman & Co.	Nisbet & Co.	Alexander Taylor.
Alexander Watt & Co.	James Maconochie.	George Downie.
William Ritchie & Co.	Weathuston & Co.	Peter Sutherland.
William Andrew.	Peter Wiseman.	William Wood.
William Ingram.	Edward Cruickshank.	John Cowie.
James Laurence & Co.	Peter Rettie.	John Donaldson.
Joseph Grant.	Alexander Carny.	George Napier.
Watt & Wiseman & Co.	William Young.	Henry Watson.
David Kennedy.	Andrew Watson.	Alexander Watson.
James Methven.	James Campbell.	**Banff**
George Wiseman.	George Paterson & Co.	Henry Munro & Co.
James Uethuen & Co.	Andrew West.	George Napier.
	James Faquharson.	James Geddes.
		James Russell.
		Munro & Morrison.

Banff Harbour early 1900's. Zulu's – 'Research', 'Reaper', and 'Renown